JAMES and the MARQUIS
the Unlikely Friendship of
Two Lafayettes

written by
LISA BOEGLIN
illustrated by
ANASTASIIA TSIPAN

Library of Congress Control Number: 2026903402

Publishing Coordinator – Clarissa Willis
Book Design – Sharon Kizziah-Holmes

Paperback: ISBN: 978-1-966675-76-1
Hardback: ISBN: 978-1-966675-77-8
E-Book ISBN: 978-1-966675-78-5

To all who believe in liberty and justice for all.

With deep appreciation for the historians (academic and interpretive) who devote themselves to uncovering and sharing the truth, no matter how complex or uncomfortable it may be. Your work ensures that our understanding of history remains honest and alive.

My heartfelt thanks to Colonial Williamsburg for your inspiring programs and steadfast commitment to your mission: "That the future may learn from the past." Your dedication reminds us that history is not only something to study, it's something to feel and carry forward. I owe special thanks to Stephen Seals, Colonial Williamsburg's interpreter of James. When I began shaping this story for children, I reached out to Stephen. He graciously read my drafts, corrected errors in my research, and shared honest, thoughtful feedback every step of the way.

And to my dear friends and family, who have cheerfully joined me on countless historical adventures and shared in my passion for the past—especially Brett, Mary, and Carrie—thank you for your patience, encouragement, and love.

Lisa Boeglin

Author's Note

In 2026, the United States celebrates 250 years of independence—a moment to honor not only famous founders like George Washington and Thomas Jefferson but also the lesser-known figures whose courage helped secure freedom. This book tells the story of two such men: James, an enslaved man who became a spy during the Revolutionary War, and the Marquis de Lafayette, a young French nobleman who crossed the ocean to fight for liberty. Their unlikely friendship helped shape history.

Over twenty years ago, I first visited Colonial Williamsburg. Walking its streets felt like stepping back in time, surrounded by reenactors portraying farmers, soldiers, shopkeepers, and enslaved people whose labor built the town. I was especially moved by a reenactment of James and Lafayette's reunion years after the war. Watching the two men—one born into slavery, the other into privilege—embrace as friends gave me chills. Later, meeting the actor who played James and learning about the real man behind the story left me wondering why his name was so little known.

James was intelligent and brave, risking his life as a spy to help win the Revolution. Lafayette, who believed deeply in liberty for all, trusted and admired him. Together, they showed that courage and honor know no color, and that the fight for justice can unite people from very different worlds.

As a teacher, I shared their story with my students, and every time the room fell silent as they leaned in, eager to learn more. Recently, renewed attention—from the American Friends of Lafayette and new historical research—has brought fresh insight into their lives and their reunion at Yorktown. Though James left no written words, his bravery still speaks. This book ensures both men are remembered and that their story of friendship, courage, and hope continues to inspire future generations.

Foreword

When I was in school, I didn't know who James Lafayette was. I always knew that all kinds of people did great things—though most never get talked about. Not every good deed gets recognized. Not every good deed is known. So, when we find out about these people who did great things, isn't it our responsibility to tell their story?

My elementary school had no books about James Lafayette. I wasn't fond of history back then. I truly wanted to love it, but there were very few stories told about American history that had characters in them who looked like me.

For more than a decade, I have had the honor of portraying James Lafayette. His story is an American story. I wonder how I might have felt about history had his story been shared with me back then. I wonder how I might have felt about my own place in this country. Would I have felt like I truly belonged? At the time, I didn't.

Had this book been in my school library, I can only imagine how it might have given me pride in my history—pride in who I am. We tell these stories so that you know: no matter who you are or what you look like; you belong. This story and this country truly belong to us all. We add to the American story every day that we live. Your very existence makes a difference. Never forget your importance to this American experiment.

I hope this book helps everyone, in some way, understand that simple yet important fact.

Stephen Seals
James Lafayette Interpreter

Before there were rock stars and sports superstars, other heroes drew cheering crowds. In 1824, forty years after the Revolutionary War, America's favorite Frenchman, General Lafayette, returned from France for a grand tour of the young nation he helped to build.

In Yorktown, Virginia, the streets hummed with excitement. Flags waved. Drums pounded. People lined the riverfront and packed the streets to see General Lafayette.

Lafayette was addressing the crowd when he spotted a familiar face. The general stopped speaking and raised his hand. The crowd hushed. Lafayette called out, “James.”

The crowd parted; a man stepped forward. Lafayette wrapped his arms around a Black man.

Two men.

Two friends.

Two Lafayettes.

One had been enslaved. The other was born into nobility. Bound by a shared victory, James Lafayette and the Marquis de Lafayette were reunited at last.

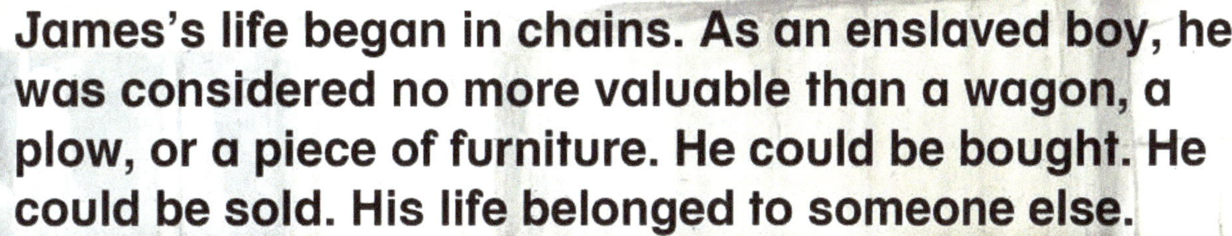

James's life began in chains. As an enslaved boy, he was considered no more valuable than a wagon, a plow, or a piece of furniture. He could be bought. He could be sold. His life belonged to someone else.

From the time James was small, white people barely noticed him. They talked around him, never to him. They carried on their business as if he wasn't there at all. For much of his life, James was invisible.

Across the ocean, young Lafayette's life was very different. Born a French nobleman, he grew up surrounded by wealth, privilege, and opportunity. He inherited a fortune and later married into one of the richest families in France. He trained in the French Royal Army, studied at the finest schools, and was celebrated in royal courts. For much of his life, Lafayette was impossible to miss.

How could two men so different forge a friendship that changed history?

Lafayette believed freedom belonged to all people, not just kings and nobles. When he heard about the American colonists' fight for liberty, he made a daring decision. Without his king's permission, he purchased a ship and sailed across the Atlantic Ocean to help the Americans.

The colonists fought for independence from Britain. But freedom for whom? Would enslaved people like James be included?

James, enslaved by William Armistead, helped transport supplies for the Virginia Army through his owner's contract to provide goods. While William managed the business as a civilian supplier, James did the demanding work, hauling barrels and crates of food and materials to the troops. During these deliveries, he first met the Marquis de Lafayette.

One day, James apologized for a mistake in a delivery.

Instead of dismissing him, Lafayette looked him in the eye and spoke to him with respect.

Why does this man see me when no one else does? James wondered.

Unlike most enslaved people, James knew how to read and write. His intelligence and honesty impressed Lafayette.

Within days, Lafayette asked William Armistead, who owned James, for permission to recruit James into his service. Armistead agreed.

Lafayette invented a daring plan. James would pretend to escape from his enslaver and offer his services to the British. The British would see only a runaway slave, not a threat. They would ignore him. His invisibility made him the perfect spy.

Hidden by night, James slipped away from home. Through forests and fields, he crept across the Virginia countryside until he reached the British lines. Soon, James became a servant in the camp of General Cornwallis, the British commander leading the fight against the American colonies.

The officers talked freely in front of James. They drew maps, whispered battle plans, and sent urgent messages. They never once imagined he was listening.

But James listened.

James watched.

James counted.

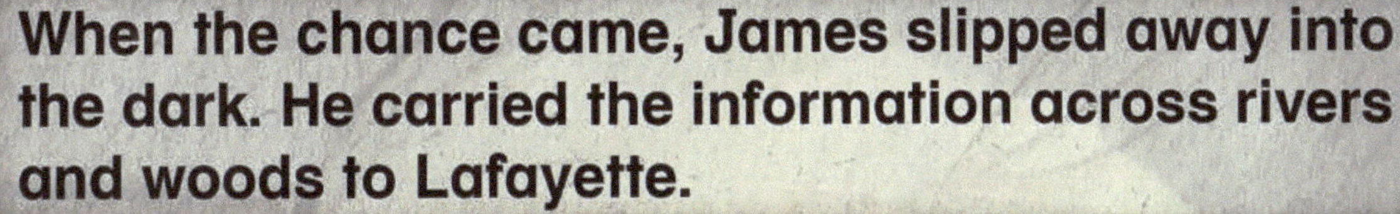

When the chance came, James slipped away into the dark. He carried the information across rivers and woods to Lafayette.

Lafayette waited.

Lafayette trusted.

Lafayette acted.

Again and again, James vanished into the wilderness, feeding Lafayette the details that could tip the balance of war in favor of the colonists.

Then, one day, Cornwallis himself summoned James. The British general needed information about the Americans. James knew the roads, rivers, and terrain. Cornwallis asked him to spy on his own countrymen.

Now James had become a double agent.

He returned to American territory as ordered. However, the information he delivered back to Cornwallis was misleading or already outdated.

There were enemies on both sides of the battlefield. Discovery meant hanging. Betrayal meant death. Still, James carried on.

At last, James uncovered Cornwallis's true plan. The British would march toward Yorktown, hoping to defeat the American rebels once and for all.

This was the intelligence report that George Washington needed to adjust his strategy and trap the British army.

The Battle of Yorktown was the turning point of the Revolutionary War. America's independence was secured. Thanks to an invisible enslaved man named James.

When the war ended, James returned home, still enslaved. His petition for freedom was denied. Only soldiers were granted liberty, not spies.

James faded back into a life of invisibility.

But Lafayette remembered. He wrote to the Virginia Assembly, praising James's courage and loyalty, urging them to honor his service.

Two long years later, James finally won his freedom. He chose a new name, James Lafayette, after the man who had seen him, trusted him, and fought beside him.

Two Lafayettes.

One celebrated, one overlooked.

Two men whose unlikely friendship helped build a new nation.

Timeline

1748 Approximate date James was born. There were no records of births for enslaved people, but other records give information to suggest the year of his birth.

1757 Lafayette was born in southern France.

1775 Lafayette learned about the rebellious colonists in America.

1776 The Declaration of Independence was written.

1777 Lafayette purchased a ship for his journey across the Atlantic ocean then set sail for America (without permission of the King) to help the colonists fight for freedom. Lafayette was contracted to become a general in the Continental Army.

1779 Lafayette went home to France.

1780 Lafayette returned to America with news of the French troops on their way to help.

1781 James met the Marquis de Lafayette. James became a spy.

1781 Battle of Yorktown was fought.
Lafayette returned to France.

1783 The Revolutionary War ends.

1784 James petitioned the Virginia General Assembly for freedom and was denied.

1786 James petitioned the Virginia General Assembly again. This time his petition is accompanied by a testimonial from the Marquis de Lafayette.

1787 The General Assembly approved the second petition. James was granted his freedom. The Virginia Assembly paid William Armistead 250 pounds sterling for the loss of his slave.

1787-1804 James paid taxes for slaves owned. It is likely that the taxes were for his children. By law, he could purchase them but could not free them until they became adults and could support themselves.

1789 The French Revolution began. Lafayette ordered the destruction of the Bastille and sent its keys to George Washington.

1792 The French monarchy was overthrown. Lafayette fled. He was captured in Austria and imprisoned for 5 years.

1797 Lafayette was freed.

1816 James purchased 40 acres of farmland.

1818 James petitioned the General Assembly to receive a pension as a soldier of the Revolutionary War. James was granted $60 immediately and received $40 annually for the rest of his life.

1824 Marquis de Lafayette returned to the United States for a national tour. He was reunited with James at Yorktown.

Timeline (Continued)

1830 James died in Baltimore, Maryland.
Lafayette took command of the French National Guard and continued to advocate for democracy.

1834 Lafayette died in France. His body is covered with American soil brought back from his farewell tour of the United States.

1891 The first memorial was erected on the southeast corner of Lafayette Park in Washington D.C. to honor Lafayette.

1997 In New Kent County, Virginia, a historic marker was erected by the Department of Historic Resources to commemorate James's contribution to the American Revolution.

2002 Congress gave honorary citizenship to Lafayette.

2024-2025 August 16, 2024, saw the kickoff of a Bicentennial celebration of Lafayette's tour of America. Hundreds of events traced Lafayette's footsteps on the exact dates and in the exact order he followed on his tour of America as the "Guest of the Nation" between 1824 and 1825.

2025 War Memorial, honoring James Lafayette, was erected by the Virginia Society Children of the American Revolution Administration and the African American Heritage Society of New Kent near the New Kent County Court House in Virginia.

Portrait of James Lafayette (1824) by John B. Martin (public domain)

Portrait of Marie-Joseph Paul Yves Roch Gilbert du Motier, Marquis de Lafayette titled *Gilbert du Motier Marquis de Lafayette (1834)* by Joseph Desire Court (public domain)

Bibliography

Websites

American Battlefield Trust https://www.battlefields.org/learn/biographies/james-armistead-lafayette
https://www.battlefields.org/learn/biographies/marquis-de-lafayette

American Revolution Museum at Yorktown
https://www.jyfmuseums.org/learn/videos/slave-spy-the-story-of-james-lafayette

Colonial Williamsburg
https://www.colonialwilliamsburg.org/discover/18th-century-people/nation-builders/james-armistead-lafayette/
https://www.colonialwilliamsburg.org/discover/18th-century-people/nation-builders/marquis-de-lafayette/

International Spy Museum
https://www.spymuseum.org/exhibition-experiences/spy-celebrates-african-america/

Lafayette 200
https://lafayette200.org/

Library of Virginia
https://edu.lva.virginia.gov/oc/stc/people/james-lafayette
https://edu.lva.virginia.gov/oc/stc/people/marquis-de-lafayette-(1757-1834)

National Archives
https://www.archives.gov/nhprc/projects/catalog/lafayette-papers

Websites (Continued)

National Museum United States Army
https://www.thenmusa.org/biographies/james-armistead-lafayette/

National Park Service
https://www.nps.gov/vafo/learn/historyculture/lafayette.htm

Our American Revolution
https://www.ouramericanrevolution.org/index.cfm/people/view/pp0053

United States Army
https://www.army.mail/article/119280/james_armistead_lafayette_1760_1832
Va 2550
https://va250.org/2024/02/16/james-armistead-lafayette-patriot-double-agent/

Books

Duncan, Mike. Hero of Two Worlds: the Marquis de Lafayette in the Age of Revolution. Public Affairs, 2021.

Grove, Tim. The World Turned Upside Down: The Yorktown Victory that Won America's Independence. Abrams Books for Young Readers, 2022.

Harrison, Vashti. Little Legends: Exceptional Men in Black History. Little,Brown and Company, 2019.

Rappaport, Doreen. Answering the Cry for Freedom: Stories of African Americans and the American Revolution. Candlewick Press, 2016.

Vowell, Sarah. Lafayette in the Somewhat United States. Riverhead Books, 2015.

Woelfe, Gretchen. Answering the Cry for Freedom : Stories of African Americans and the American Revolution. Calkins Creek, 2016.

Primary Sources

https://rosetta.virginiamemory.com/delivery/DeliveryManagerServlet?dps_pid=IE2859042
Petition by James

https://thevalentine.org/explore/richmond-stories/featured-stories/the-revolutionary-james-fayette/ various articles and documents including letter from Lafayette

https://www.loc.gov/resource/sn84024735/1824-10-29/ed-1/?sp=3&st=image&r=0.189,0.784,0.891,0.426,0 Richmond Enquirer, 29 Oct. 1824, p. 3, Library of Congress.

Colonial Williamsburg Nation Builders Interpreters; Williamsburg, Va

Legacy of the Lafayettes

This historical marker and monument, as a tribute to James, is in New Kent County, Virginia.

The historical marker and the "Four Heroes of Yorktown" monument are in Yorktown, Virginia.

About the Author
Lisa Boeglin

Lisa is a former Indiana PTA Teacher of the Year, lover of nature, artist, traveler, and proud bat nerd. A history enthusiast and storyteller at heart, Lisa has adopted the title of "Unofficial, Self-Appointed, Ambassador to Colonial Williamsburg". She now lives in southern Indiana with her husband and their rotten fur-baby. She's the proud mom of four adult children and "BeeBee" to two precious grandchildren.

From the moment she began reading picture books aloud to her students, Lisa dreamed of seeing her own name on a cover—bringing stories to life for young readers everywhere.

A retired elementary teacher with a master's degree in Early Childhood Education, Lisa continues to inspire future educators as an adjunct instructor at a local community college. When she's not writing or spending time with her grandkids, you'll find her exploring new places, cheering on the Indiana Hoosiers, or tucked away in her Evansville home, crafting picture books filled with heart, history, and wonder.

About the Illustrator
Anastasiia Tsipan

Anastasiia is an illustrator from Ukraine. Drawing is something that has accompanied her since childhood. While studying at school, and later at university, she always tried to find time to draw. Even now, with three young children, she still finds time to create new illustrations. Anastasiia is a speech therapist by profession. But during her maternity leave, she realized she needed to practice and develop her God-given talent. Anastasiia wants to do something good for others, so her illustrations convey friendship, kindness, joy, and love, because this is very necessary for this world.

www.ingramcontent.com/pod-product-compliance
Lightning Source LLC
LaVergne TN
LVHW070159110826
845147LV00002B/445
* 9 7 8 1 9 6 6 6 7 5 7 6 1 *